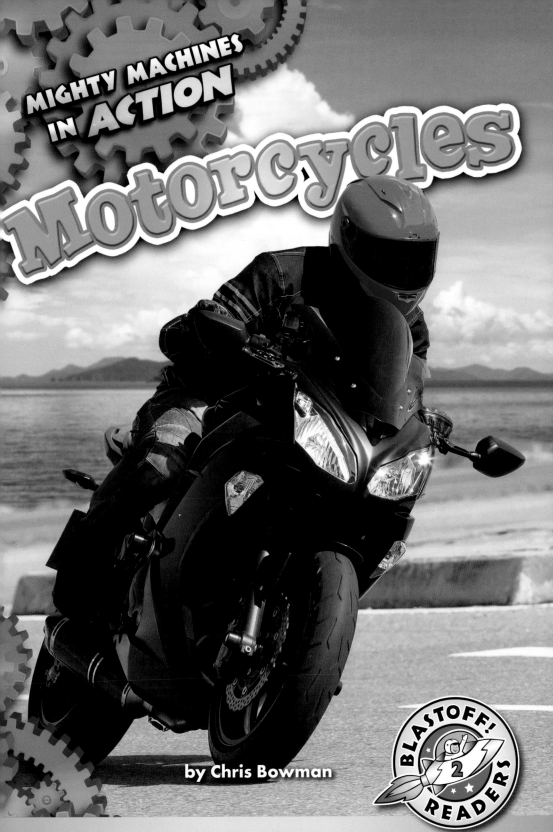

MIGHTY MACHINES IN ACTION

Motorcycles

by Chris Bowman

BELLWETHER MEDIA • MINNEAPOLIS, MN

Note to Librarians, Teachers, and Parents:

Blastoff! Readers are carefully developed by literacy experts and combine standards-based content with developmentally appropriate text.

Level 1 provides the most support through repetition of high-frequency words, light text, predictable sentence patterns, and strong visual support.

Level 2 offers early readers a bit more challenge through varied simple sentences, increased text load, and less repetition of high-frequency words.

Level 3 advances early-fluent readers toward fluency through increased text and concept load, less reliance on visuals, longer sentences, and more literary language.

Level 4 builds reading stamina by providing more text per page, increased use of punctuation, greater variation in sentence patterns, and increasingly challenging vocabulary.

Level 5 encourages children to move from "learning to read" to "reading to learn" by providing even more text, varied writing styles, and less familiar topics.

Whichever book is right for your reader, Blastoff! Readers are the perfect books to build confidence and encourage a love of reading that will last a lifetime!

This edition first published in 2018 by Bellwether Media, Inc.

No part of this publication may be reproduced in whole or in part without written permission of the publisher. For information regarding permission, write to Bellwether Media, Inc., Attention: Permissions Department, 5357 Penn Avenue South, Minneapolis, MN 55419.

Library of Congress Cataloging-in-Publication Data

Names: Bowman, Chris, 1990- author.
Title: Motorcycles / by Chris Bowman.
Description: Minneapolis, MN : Bellwether Media, Inc., 2018. | Series: Blastoff! Readers: Mighty Machines in Action | Includes bibliographical references and index. | Audience: Ages 5-8. | Audience: K to Grade 3.
Identifiers: LCCN 2017031302 (print) | LCCN 2017032236 (ebook) | ISBN 9781626177581 (hardcover : alk. paper) | ISBN 9781681034638 (ebook)
Subjects: LCSH: Motorcycles–Juvenile literature.
Classification: LCC TL440.15 (ebook) | LCC TL440.15 .B69 2018 (print) | DDC 629.227/5–dc23
LC record for Motorcycles available at https://lccn.loc.gov/2017031302

Editor: Rebecca Sabelko   Designer: Steve Porter

Printed in the United States of America, North Mankato, MN.

Table of Contents

A SMOOTH RIDE

The sun begins to set. A rider puts on her helmet and climbs onto her motorcycle.

She **revs** the engine and zooms down the road.

The rider enjoys the view as she cruises by.

What a perfect evening
for a motorcycle ride!

MOTORCYCLE MANIA!

cruiser

Motorcycles may be found zipping down highways or speeding on trails. They are built to go many places!

Standard motorcycles are popular for new riders. **Cruisers** have low seats and high handlebars.

COMMON MOTORCYCLES

standard:
2017 Yamaha XSR900

cruiser:
2017 Harley-Davidson
Dyna Street Bob

Some motorcycles are built for speed. **Sportbikes** often weigh less and go faster than other motorcycles.

sportbike

touring
motorcycle

Touring motorcycles are meant for long rides. They have big gas tanks and powerful engines.

Dirt bikes ride on rough roads.
They can go almost anywhere.

dirt bike

2015 KAWASAKI NINJA H2

type: sportbike

top speed: 183 miles (295 kilometers) per hour

0 to 60 time: 2.6 seconds

Dual-sport motorcycles look like dirt bikes. But they ride on and off roads.

HANDLEBARS, ENGINES, AND WHEELS

Riders **steer** with the handlebars. These can be low or high on the bike.

handlebars

leaning

Leaning also helps riders change direction.

Motorcycle engines have one to six **cylinders**.

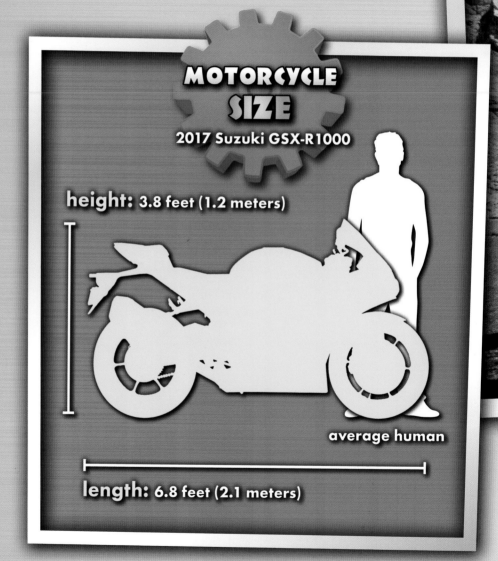

MOTORCYCLE SIZE

2017 Suzuki GSX-R1000

height: 3.8 feet (1.2 meters)

average human

length: 6.8 feet (2.1 meters)

engine

Bigger engines allow bikes
to gain speed quickly.

knobby tires

Most motorcycles have two wheels. Those that ride on streets often have smooth tires.

Dirt bikes have thick, **knobby** tires.

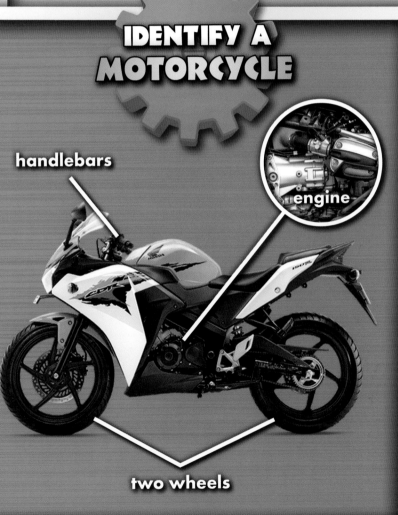

IDENTIFY A MOTORCYCLE

handlebars

engine

two wheels

TAKE A SPIN

Motorcycles come in all shapes and sizes. Riders continue to enjoy their many uses.

No matter where a rider wants to go, there is a motorcycle for the job!

Glossary

cruisers—motorcycles with low seats and high handlebars; cruisers are sometimes called "choppers."

cylinders—parts of an engine where gas is burned

dirt bikes—motorcycles that are able to ride off roads and over jumps

dual-sport motorcycles—motorcycles that can ride on or off roads

knobby—bumpy

leaning—tipping the body to the side

revs—turns a part of the engine; the engine makes a noise when it revs.

sportbikes—motorcycles built for speed; sportbikes have high foot pegs and low handlebars that make riders bend forward.

standard motorcycles—motorcycles that allow riders to sit up straight

steer—to control movement

touring motorcycles—big motorcycles that are comfortable to ride for long distances; touring motorcycles also have places to store the riders' bags.

To Learn More

AT THE LIBRARY

Graham, Ian. *Bikes*. Buffalo, N.Y.: Firefly, 2017.

Riggs, Kate. *Motorcycles*. Mankato, Minn.: Creative Education, 2015.

Schuh, Mari. *Motorcycles*. North Mankato, Minn.: Capstone Press, 2017.

ON THE WEB

Learning more about motorcycles is as easy as 1, 2, 3.

1. Go to www.factsurfer.com.

2. Enter "motorcycles" into the search box.

3. Click the "Surf" button and you will see a list of related web sites.

With factsurfer.com, finding more information is just a click away.

Index